THE IROQUOIS

BY CHARLOTTE WILCOX

CONSULTANT: MIKE WAHRARE TARBELL
AN AKWESASNE MOHAWK OF THE TURTLE CLAN AND EDUCATOR AT
THE IROQUOIS INDIAN MUSEUM IN HOWES CAVE, NEW YORK

LERNER PUBLICATIONS COMPANY
MINNEAPOLIS

ABOUT THE COVER IMAGE: The Great Chain (Covenant Belt) marked a 1794 treaty between the Iroquois Confederacy and the United States. The figures on the belt represent a chain of friendship between the Iroquois and the first thirteen U.S. states.

PHOTO ACKNOWLEDGMENTS:
The images in this book are used with the permission of: Peabody Museum, Harvard University (90-17-10/49318 T1683.1), backgrounds on pp. 1, 3, 4, 18, 28, 42; © Archivo Icongrafico, S.A./CORBIS, p. 6; Courtesy of the New York State Museum, Albany, NY, pp. 8, 25; Courtesy of the Division of Anthropology, American Museum of Natural History, p. 9 (50/6208), 11 (50/6238 AB); © MPI/Getty Images, pp. 10, 19, 22, 24; 26; Francis Lee Jaques, Minnesota Historical Society Art Collection, p. 13; PhotoDisc Royalty Free by Getty Images, p. 14; © Bettmann/CORBIS, pp. 15, 20, 38, 40; courtesy of the Library of Congress, pp. 16, 33, 35, 36, 37, 41; © Newberry Library/ SuperStock, p. 21; John Kahionhes Fadden, p. 23; Hiawatha Wampum Belt, NYSM reference number E-37309; now curated at The Onondaga Nation.   Photo courtesy of New York State Museum, used with permission of The Council of Chiefs, Onondaga Nation, p. 27; Confederation Life Gallery of Canadian History, p. 29; Harold R. Walters/American Museum of Natural History (#3376004), p. 30; © CORBIS, pp. 31, 49; © Pat and Chuck Blackley, p. 34; Ernie Smith, *The Hunter,* 1938, (detail), Rochester Museum and Science Center Department of Collections, p. 39; © Lawrence D. Migdale/Mira.com, p. 43; AP/Wide World Photos, pp. 44, 45; Green Bay Visitor & Convention Bureau, p. 47; © Lawrence Migdale/ Photo Researchers, Inc., 50.
Cover: Washington Covenant Belt, NYSM reference number E-37310; now curated at the Onondaga Nation. Photo courtesy of New York State Museum, used with permission of The Council of Chiefs, Onondaga Nation.

Lerner Publications Company
A division of Lerner Publishing Group
241 First Avenue North
Minneapolis, MN 55401 U.S.A.

Website address: www.lernerbooks.com

Library of Congress Cataloging-in-Publication Data

Wilcox, Charlotte.
    The Iroquois / by Charlotte Wilcox.
      p.   cm. — (Native American histories)
    Includes bibliographical references and index.
    ISBN-13: 978-0-8225-2637-7 (lib. bdg. : alk. paper)
    ISBN-10: 0-8225-2637-9 (lib. bdg. : alk. paper)
      1. Iroquois Indians—History. 2. Iroquois Indians—Social life and customs.
    3. Six Nations. I. Title. II. Series.
    E99.I7W54 2007
    974.7004'9755—dc22   2004029288

Manufactured in the United States of America
1 2 3 4 5 6 – BP – 12 11 10 09 08 07

CONTENTS

CHAPTER 1

THE SIX NATIONS

THE IROQUOIS ARE NATIVE AMERICANS, SOMETIMES CALLED AMERICAN INDIANS. Native Americans have lived in North America for thousands of years. The Iroquois homeland is in modern-day New York State.

Six separate groups, called nations, make up the Iroquois. The nations are the Mohawk, Oneida, Onondaga, Cayuga, Seneca, and Tuscarora. Each of these nations is more than a thousand years old. Each nation has its own government.

Early French settlers called the people belonging to these nations the Iroquois. Their government was called the Iroquois Confederacy. The Iroquois call themselves Haudenosaunee, meaning "People Building a Longhouse." (A longhouse is a traditional Iroquois home.) The Haudenosaunees' modern government is called the Six Nations.

THE IROQUOIS LANGUAGE

The Iroquois are part of a larger group of Native Americans who speak the same type of language. This language type is called the Iroquois family of languages. The Cherokee and Huron Indians also belong to this group. Each nation has its own language, but the languages share many sounds and words.

COMMUNITY LIFE

For many centuries, the Iroquois lived in villages surrounded by tall wooden fences. Smaller villages had a few hundred people. Many thousands of people lived in the large towns.

Fields of corn, beans, and squash surrounded the villages and towns. Some fields were many miles long. The Iroquois also grew apple and peach trees. They ate fish and meat from deer, beaver, geese,

Iroquois villages looked much like this Pomeioc Indian village. A tall wooden fence surrounds the longhouses. Fields and water are nearby.

THE THREE SISTERS

Corn, beans, and squash crops supplied most of the food for Iroquois villages. The Iroquois believed that the plants were special gifts from the Creator. Each plant was protected by one of three sister spirits. To honor those spirits, the Iroquois called the plants the Three Sisters.

Iroquois women planted the crops together, and each plant worked to help the other grow. The beans provided the soil with special nutrients. The cornstalks served as poles for the growing beans. And the leafy squash plants shaded the ground, keeping the soil moist.

and other animals. The women usually raised the crops. The men did the hunting and fishing.

Inside the village fences stood rows of longhouses. Longhouses were built of wood frames covered with tree bark. A longhouse was usually 50 to 100 feet long and about 28 feet wide. But some longhouses were more than 200 feet long.

A longhouse was like an apartment building. Most longhouses were home to about five families. A large one could hold twenty-five families.

Inside the longhouse, each family had its own living space. They had a fire pit for cooking and for heat. The walls were lined with shelves for storing food and supplies. In summer, the family slept on benches. In colder weather, the family slept on floor mats close to the fire.

Several families lived in a longhouse. But each family had its own living area. The homes provided sturdy shelter for the families.

Braided corn husks keep ears of corn together for drying.
The Iroquois also braided corn husks to make clothing and shoes.

CLOTHING AND FOOTWEAR

Early Iroquois people made their clothes and shoes from natural items. They used furs, leather, braided tree or plant fibers, and corn husks. They decorated their clothing with feathers, quills, seashells, or beads made of seeds.

The men and boys wore breechcloths or kilts. Breechcloths were like shorts made of leather. A kilt is a short skirt worn by a man.

In cool weather, men wore leather shirts with fringes. In warm weather, they wore brightly decorated sashes over their shoulders or large bead or quill neckpieces.

Women wore long tops, called overdresses, with skirts beneath. The dresses and skirts were made of leather, trimmed with quills and beads. Both men and women often wore leggings made of leather. Leggings are like pants with no tops. They cover the legs from the thighs to the ankles. In winter, everyone also wore fur robes.

The Iroquois woman at left is wearing a leather skirt. The warrior at right is wearing armor made from elm bark and woven plant fibers. Leggings cover his legs.

These moccasins are made from leather and decorated with beads. The Iroquois also made footwear from corn husks and other materials.

Moccasins, a type of shoe, were made of leather or corn husks. The moccasins were decorated with beads, quills, or tassels.

Both Iroquois men and women wore beautiful headwear with many decorations. Each of the six Iroquois nations had a different way of attaching feathers to their headwear. This was one way the Iroquois showed pride in their nation. It also was a way for others to recognize someone from a different nation.

When Europeans first arrived in North America in the 1500s, they brought with them cotton and wool cloth. The Iroquois began trading with the Europeans for the soft, brightly colored fabrics to make clothing.

The European traders also brought glass beads. The Iroquois combined the beads with their clothing. They used them with furs, leather, plant fibers, shells, and quills.

The styles were the same, but the cloth and beads gave the clothing a new look. Some Iroquois still wear these clothing styles for special occasions.

THE MEANINGS OF THE SIX NATIONS

MOHAWK	People of the Crystals
ONEIDA	People of the Standing Stone
ONONDAGA	People of the Hills
CAYUGA	People of the Marshland
SENECA	People of the Great Hill
TUSCARORA	People Wearing Shirts

French fur traders traveled rivers in North America. They traded goods, such as cotton cloth, with the Iroquois and others.

IROQUOIS BELIEFS

Europeans also brought the Christian religion to North America. Many Iroquois became Christians over time, but they still honored their people's traditions.

Iroquois beliefs and traditions are ancient. They were handed down through many generations. These beliefs and traditions were practiced as part of daily life in the villages and towns.

The Iroquois believe that there is a living spirit in all things. It is in animals, such as hawks.

The Iroquois believe that a creator made all things. They also believe that there is a living spirit in all things. This includes animals, plants, rocks, water, and winds. Living at peace with other people and with nature is part of Iroquois life.

Being thankful to the Creator is also part of the Iroquois way of life. The Cycle of Thanksgiving reflects this. Throughout the year, the Iroquois give thanks for the gifts of the Creator and of nature. During some festivals in the cycle, the Iroquois honor their ancestors. Other festivals celebrate the ripening or harvesting of foods. In still other celebrations, the Iroquois thank the sun and the moon.

The Iroquois value kindness and sharing. In their traditional communities, everyone took part in planting, hunting, making clothes, and cooking food. And everyone benefited from that work.

This old drawing shows Mohawk people doing a day's work. The Iroquois each shared the work that had to be done each day.

THE CLANS

Iroquois life is centered on the family. Each family belongs to a group of families called a clan. A clan is a group of families that all come from the same ancestor. Nine clans form the Iroquois nations.

A clan is led by a head clan mother. In clan elections, she has the power to name candidates for chief. She also has the power to remove chiefs from office.

Members of this Iroquois clan posed for this photograph in the early 1900s. Each member of this clan came from a shared ancestor.

CLANS

Clan loyalty is still very important to Iroquois people. The clans are named after animals. For example, there are Heron, Hawk, Snipe, Deer, Eel, Beaver, Turtle, Bear, and Wolf clans. When a man and woman become partners of life, the man lives in the woman's house. Children will belong to their mother's clan.

The chiefs have subchiefs to help them carry out their duties for the people. The clan mother also chooses her war captain. That person answers only to her and is at her call at all times. Faithkeepers help her conduct ceremonies at their proper times throughout the year.

Clan mothers, chiefs, and faithkeepers serve in their positions for life. They are asked or told to give up their roles only if they commit a crime. When a chief dies or leaves, the clan mother selects a new chief. The new chief must be approved by the nation's other leaders.

CHAPTER 2

A MESSAGE OF PEACE

THE HISTORY OF THE IROQUOIS PEOPLE HAS BEEN HANDED DOWN TO THEM BY THEIR ANCESTORS. One of the most important parts of Iroquois history concerns a Huron man called the Peacemaker.

About a thousand years ago, the Iroquois were not getting along. Families, villages, and nations fought against each other. There was much killing and suffering. Then the Peacemaker began spreading a message of peace from the Creator. The Creator wanted the people to stop fighting and unite in peace.

The Peacemaker came to a place where he could gather his strength for all the work that he had to do. This place was the house of a woman he would call Jegonsahseh, "The New Face."

The Peacemaker was a Huron man who spread a message of peace from the Creator.

The Peacemaker told her his dream for the Great Peace. Jegonsahseh embraced his dream, and she would become known as the Mother of Nations. Then the Peacemaker began his work among the Mohawks.

In his travels, the Peacemaker also came across Hiawatha, an Onondaga man. Hiawatha was a great warrior, who was grieving the death of his daughters. The Peacemaker's message touched Hiawatha's heart. Hiawatha began to help the Peacemaker spread his message.

Hiawatha *(left)* speaks to a young Iroquois boy. Hiawatha helped the Peacemaker spread the message of peace.

Hiawatha used shell wampum belts like these to record the Peacemaker's message. He then shared the belts' messages of peace with the Iroquois.

The Iroquois did not use books or letters to communicate. So Hiawatha invented a way to record messages. He used strings of colored seashells, called wampum. Hiawatha wove the wampum into belts. The belts could be used to remember a message or recall an important event.

Hiawatha taught some Mohawks how to record the Peacemaker's message on wampum belts. The belts helped spread the message among the Mohawks. They became the first nation to accept the message of peace.

Tododaho sits smoking a pipe. He did not like the Peacemaker's plan.

The Peacemaker and Hiawatha spread their message to other Iroquois nations for many years. The Cayuga, Oneida, and Seneca finally believed too.

But an Onondaga man named Tododaho was against the Peacemaker and Hiawatha. Tododaho had a twisted body and wore snakes in his hair. He did not want peace among the nations. He used all his powers to keep people from accepting the Peacemaker's message. But the Peacemaker would not let Tododaho stand in the way. The Peacemaker had a plan.

THE GREAT LAW OF PEACE

The Peacemaker invited Mohawk, Oneida, Cayuga, and Seneca leaders to a meeting. The Peacemaker urged the leaders to form a confederacy, or a union of nations. Instead of fighting, the confederacy would solve problems by talking. The nations would be bound to each other by the Great Law of Peace.

Iroquois leaders meet at the first Grand Council to talk about the Peacemaker's Great Law of Peace. They form a united group, called the Iroquois Confederacy.

Each nation, the Peacemaker said, would choose chiefs to sit on a council. The council would be the nation's government. It would decide the best ways to act on behalf of the people of the nation. Each nation was to keep a council fire burning in a village in the center of their territory.

Each nation's council would also select chiefs to speak for the nation at a grand council. The Grand Council would be a government made up of all the nations in the confederacy. The Grand Council

This tribe mark shows the Peacemaker's plan for the Iroquois Confederacy. Four nations surround a center nation. It is also the undying council fire.

The Peacemaker used the example of a longhouse to explain how a united, peaceful Iroquois Confederacy could work.

chiefs would solve problems between nations and prevent war.

The Peacemaker used a longhouse to show the meaning of his message. In a longhouse, several families live together. Each family has its own home, but the families live under one roof. Several nations could come together in the same way. Each nation would have its separate lands and leadership. But they would all live under one law. The imagined Iroquois longhouse would stretch from Mohawk lands in the east to Seneca lands in the west.

TODODAHO JOINS THE CHIEFS

All of the chiefs agreed with the Peacemaker's plan. After the meeting, they went to Tododaho's house singing a song of peace. Tododaho came out of his house shouting angrily. But then he began to listen.

The Peacemaker offered to make Tododaho a chief in the new confederacy. He told Tododaho that the Grand Council would meet on Onondaga land.

Hiawatha *(left)* and the Peacemaker *(center)* ask Tododaho to accept the peace plan and offer to make him a chief.

On Hiawatha's belt, the squares stand for *(from left to right)* the Seneca, the Cayuga, the Oneida, and the Mohawk. The Onondaga are represented by the Tree of Peace in the center.

At last, Tododaho accepted the message. The snakes were combed from his hair, and his twisted body stood up straight and tall.

That day, the Grand Council stood in a circle and planted a Tree of Peace. They buried their weapons of war under the tree. They lit a council fire that was never to go out. The Iroquois Confederacy was born with five nations.

Hiawatha made a wampum belt to record the historic event. It showed five figures, standing for the first five nations of the confederacy.

CHAPTER 3

TIMES OF CHANGE

THE GREAT LAW OF PEACE ENDED MUCH OF THE FIGHTING AMONG IROQUOIS NATIONS.

The Grand Council began to settle arguments. The Grand Council had fifty chiefs. Ten were Cayuga, nine were Mohawk, and nine were Oneida. Fourteen chiefs were Onondaga, and eight were Seneca. The chiefs met around the council fire near modern-day Syracuse, New York.

After the Great Law was adopted, the Iroquois Confederacy grew strong. By the end of the 1400s, Iroquois land covered most of modern New York State and parts of northern Pennsylvania and southern Ontario, Canada.

THE ARRIVAL OF EUROPEANS

In the early 1500s, explorers and traders from Europe arrived in North America. French and English traders brought guns, iron cooking pots, and other tools. The Iroquois traded furs for these items and made friendships with the traders.

Explorer John Cabot *(left)* claims land for King Henry VII of England. Cabot arrived in Canada around 1500. More Europeans followed and claimed Native American lands for their countries.

But the traders also brought harmful diseases, such as smallpox and influenza. Native Americans had never been exposed to these illnesses. Their bodies could not fight them off. Hundreds of thousands of Iroquois and other Native Americans grew sick and died.

The European settlers eventually caused other serious problems. In the 1600s, people from England, Holland, and France began flooding into Iroquois territory. These settlers tried to take Iroquois land to start farms and build towns.

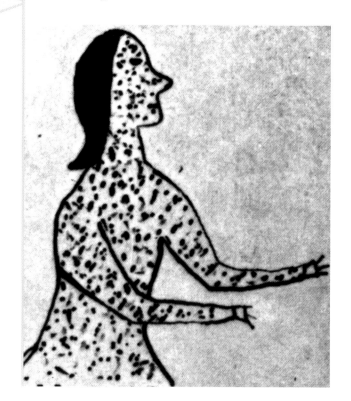

This drawing shows a Native American man who has the measles. The disease, brought by Europeans, was deadly to many Native Americans.

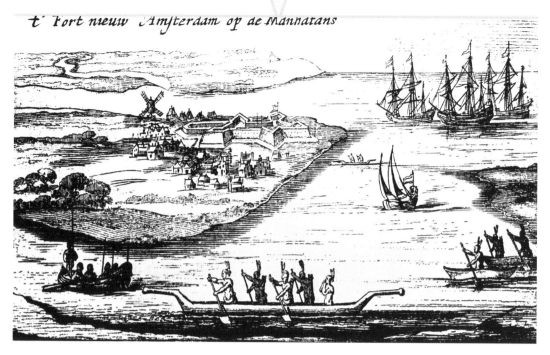

The Dutch settlement of New Amsterdam was built on Iroquois territory in the early 1650s. It later became New York City.

Some Iroquois fought hard against the settlers. A few Iroquois groups went north into territories held by other Native American nations. The Iroquois then fought with these nations over control of the land. The fighting continued for many years. But soon, greater wars would begin.

THE AMERICAN REVOLUTION

In the mid-1700s, Great Britain controlled most of the land along the eastern coast of North America. This territory was known as the American colonies.

France controlled a large strip of land west of the American colonies. It ran from the Great Lakes to the Gulf of Mexico. As the colonies grew, colonists moved west into French and Native American

THE SIXTH NATION

The Tuscarora Nation did not live near the first five nations. The Tuscarora lived in modern-day North Carolina. But like the other nations, they lived in longhouses and spoke an Iroquois language.

In the early 1700s, white settlers began forcing the Tuscaroras out of their homeland. When the Tuscaroras asked for help, the Oneidas welcomed them onto Oneida land in New York. The Tuscaroras joined the Iroquois Confederacy around 1722, and the confederacy became known as the Six Nations.

Because the Tuscarora Nation was not a member of the confederacy when the Great Law of Peace was adopted, their chiefs do not sit on the Grand Council. Instead, the Cayuga and Oneida chiefs speak for the Tuscarora people on the Grand Council.

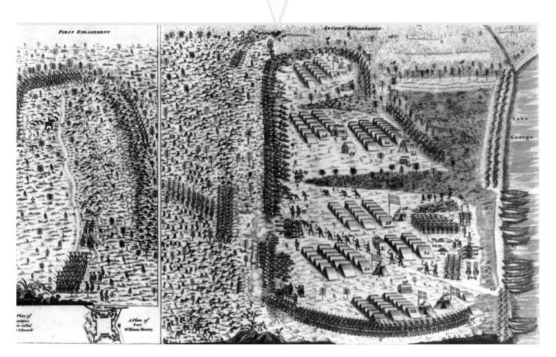

British and Mohawk warriors *(right)* defeat French and Native American forces during the Battle of Lake George in 1755.

territories. The French and the Native Americans wanted to keep the colonists out.

From 1754 to 1763, the British army and the American colonists fought against the French army. Both sides drew Native Americans, including many Iroquois, into the fighting. This fighting was called the French and Indian War. Much of the war took place along the modern border between the United States and Canada. This area was the heart of Iroquois territory. In the end, Great Britain won and took control of much more land.

American colonists had fought on the side of Great Britain in the French and Indian War. But in the years after the war, American colonists grew unhappy with being ruled by Great Britain. The colonists began to rebel. In 1775 the rebellion turned into the American Revolution.

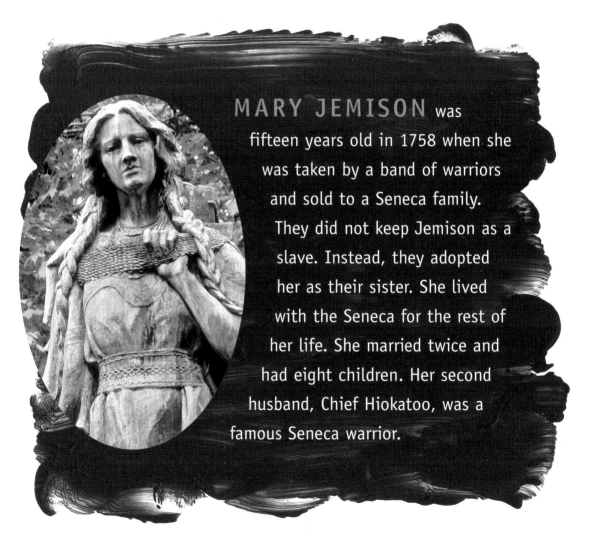

MARY JEMISON was fifteen years old in 1758 when she was taken by a band of warriors and sold to a Seneca family. They did not keep Jemison as a slave. Instead, they adopted her as their sister. She lived with the Seneca for the rest of her life. She married twice and had eight children. Her second husband, Chief Hiokatoo, was a famous Seneca warrior.

Some Mohawk leaders, such as Tiyanoka *(right, in British uniform)*, and their their people joined the British during the French and Indian War. Other Mohawk chiefs later fought for the British during the American Revolution (1775–1783).

During the Revolution, both the British and the Americans wanted the Iroquois to fight on their side. At first, the Iroquois did not want to take sides. But as the war spread, the Iroquois were drawn into the fighting.

Most warriors of the Mohawk and Seneca nations fought for Great Britain. They were led by Mohawk chief Joseph Brant and Seneca chief Sayenqueraghta (Old Smoke). The Oneida and Tuscarora, both led by Skenandoah, fought for the Americans. This split caused bad feelings among the Iroquois that took many years to heal.

JOSEPH BRANT, Thayendanegea, led Mohawk and Seneca warriors. They fought for the British in the American Revolution. After the war, the British gave Brant's people land in Ontario, Canada. The town of Brantford, Ontario, was named for him. Later, Brant traveled across North America trying to start a confederacy of all Native Americans. Like other Iroquois, he became a Christian after contact with white people. He also worked on translating the Christian Bible into Mohawk.

After the American colonists won the war in 1783, the Americans formed a new government. The colonies became states, together called the United States of America. Benjamin Franklin was an important leader in the new government. Franklin used the Six Nations as a model for the

United States. Franklin believed the Six Nations showed how many states could work together under one government.

Because some of the Iroquois helped win the American Revolution, U.S. president George Washington made a peace treaty, or agreement, with the Six Nations. The United States and the Six Nations were to live together side by side. They made a wampum belt to record the treaty.

Leaders of the Six Nations signed this peace treaty with the U.S. government in 1784.

ARTICLES of a TREATY,

Concluded at FORT STANWIX, on the twenty-second day of October, one thousand seven hundred and eighty-four, between Oliver Wolcott, Richard Butler and Arthur Lee, COMMISSIONERS PLENIPOTENTIARY from the United States in Congress assembled, on the one Part, and the SACHEMS and WARRIORS of the SIX NATIONS on the other.

THE United States of America give peace to the Senecas, Mohawks, Onondagas and Cayugas, and receive them into their protection upon the following conditions.

Article 1. Six hostages shall be immediately delivered to the commissioners by the said nations, to remain in possession of the United States, till all the prisoners white and black, which were taken by the said Senecas, Mohawks, Onondagas and Cayugas, or by any of them in the late war, from among the people of the United States, shall be delivered up.

Art. 2. The Oneida and Tuscarora nations shall be secured in the possession of the lands on which they are settled.

Art. 3. A line shall be drawn, beginning at the mouth of a creek about four miles east of Niagara, called Oyonwayea or Johnson's Landing Place, upon the lake named by the Indians Oswego, and by its Ontario, from thence southerly in a direction always four miles east of the carrying path, between lake Erie and Ontario, to the mouth of Tehoseroron or Buffalo creek on lake Erie, thence south to the north boundary of the state of Pennsylvania, thence west to the end of the said north boundary, thence south along the west boundary of the said state, to the river Ohio, the said line from the mouth of the Oyonwayea to the Ohio, shall be the western boundary of the lands of the Six Nations, so that the Six Nations shall and do yield to the United States, all claims to the country west of the said boundary, and then they shall be secured in the peaceful possession of the lands they inhabit east and north of the same, referring only six miles square round the fort of Oswego, to the United States, for the support of the same.

Art. 4. The Commissioners of the United States in consideration of the present circumstances of the Six Nations, and in execution of the humane and liberal views of the United States upon the signing of the above articles, will order goods to be delivered to the said Six Nations for their use and comfort.

Mohawks,
ONOGWENDAHONJI, his ✕ ( ) mark.
TORWIGHNATOGON, his ✕ ( ) mark.

OLIVER WOLCOTT,   (L.S.)
RICHARD BUTLER,   (L.S.)
ARTHUR LEE,   (L.S.)

Onondagas,
OHBADARIGHTON, his ✕ ( ) mark.
KENDARINDGON, his ✕ ( ) mark.

Senecas,
TAYAGONENDAGIGHTI, his ✕ ( ) mark.
TEHONWAEAGHRIYAGI, his ✕ ( ) mark.

[Signers carried forward.]

OTYADONENGHTI,

CORNPLANTER

was the son of a Dutch trader and a Seneca woman of the Wolf clan. When the American Revolution began, Cornplanter did not want the Seneca to fight. But at a meeting in 1777, other Seneca people voted to side with the British. Cornplanter felt he had to honor the voters' wishes. After the war was over, Cornplanter believed that it would be best for his people to make peace with the new U.S. government. For the rest of his time as a Seneca chief, he urged his people to act in peace. Cornplanter was said to be one hundred years old when he died in Pennsylvania in 1836.

BROKEN PROMISES

The United States then made several other treaties with the nations. The Six Nations believed the United States would not try to take Iroquois lands. The United States and the Six Nations had promised to respect each other's borders.

But New York State did not see things that way. The state took pieces of Iroquois land and gave it to land dealers. The land dealers made lots of money selling it to settlers. The settlers continued to take even more Iroquois land. Soon almost half the Iroquois were forced out of their homelands. Most settled just across the border in Canada.

An Iroquois hunter prepares to shoot a deer. The Six Nations had less room to hunt and grow crops as more Americans settled on Iroquois lands.

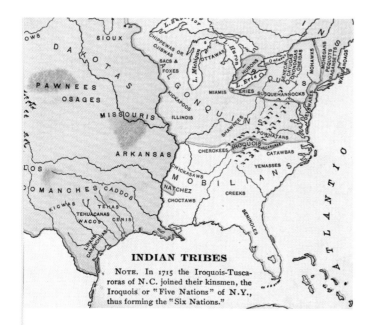

This map shows the traditional homelands of many Native American peoples. The homeland of the Iroquois, including the Oneida Nation, is shaded pink.

THE ONEIDA

Before the American Revolution, the Oneida Nation had a large territory. It covered about six million acres in New York State. Like other Iroquois nations, the Oneida lost most of this land to settlers. On what land was left, the Oneida took in some smaller Native American tribes that had been driven off their lands.

In about 1820, a rich land dealer offered the Oneida a trade for their land in New York State. The land dealer paid travel expenses for some Oneida to visit Wisconsin. The Oneida ended up trading goods for 65,400 acres of land near Green Bay, Wisconsin.

Not all Oneida people wanted to go to Wisconsin. During the 1820s and 1830s, about 650 Oneida moved to Wisconsin. A small group moved to Ontario, Canada. Another group moved onto an Onondaga reservation near Syracuse, New York. The U.S. government set aside this land for use by the Native American group. The last group refused to leave their homeland. They stayed on a small piece of their land near Oneida, New York. The Oneida Nation was broken into four parts.

Land dealers and settlers moved into New York state and forced the Oneida nation off their lands.

CHAPTER 4

KEEPING the FIRE BURNING

THE SIX NATIONS ONCE LIVED CLOSE ENOUGH TOGETHER TO FORM THE GREAT LONGHOUSE. But the modern members of the Six Nations are scattered over parts of North America. Even so, they are united and call themselves the Haudenosaunee.

About 76,000 Haudenosaunee live in North
America. Of those, about 46,000 live in the
Canadian provinces of Ontario and Quebec. The
rest live in the United States. About 17,500 live
in New York State, more than 10,000 live in
Wisconsin, and almost 2,500 live in Oklahoma.

A few Haudenosaunee still live on part of the
lands of their ancestors. These lands were never
taken over by the U.S. or the Canadian government.

This Onondaga family lives on the Iroquois reservation at Nedrow, New
York. They are among the 17,500 Iroquois living in that state.

The Wisconsin Oneida recently built this elementary school on its reservation. Many Oneida children study Iroquois languages at school.

Other Haudenosaunee lands are Indian reservations. The Wisconsin Oneida live on reservation land they purchased from other Native Americans. A group of Cayuga and Seneca moved to a reservation in Oklahoma in 1831.

THE MODERN GRAND COUNCIL

After more than eight hundred years, the Grand Council still meets around the council fire on Onondaga land near Syracuse. Members of each nation's councils elect the fifty chiefs. The chiefs make decisions for their people.

Each of the Six Nations also continues to have its own national government. The councils of chiefs and clan mothers meet in the longhouses to carry out government business. They provide public safety, education, health care, and community services. They issue passports and licenses and make their own laws.

The Canadian Haudenosaunee have their own Grand Council. They also attend the official Grand Council meetings in New York State.

Haudenosaunee chiefs, clan mothers, and faithkeepers continue to follow the path of the Peacemaker. They keep their people united and working for common goals.

Marilyn John is a clan mother of the Bear Clan. Iroquois chiefs, clan mothers, and faith-keepers continue to live by the Great Law of Peace.

THE GAME OF LACROSSE

Many Native American groups played games with sticks and balls. A Haudenosaunee stickball game became the modern sport of lacrosse. On lacrosse teams, each player carries a stick with a small net on the end. Players throw, carry, and catch the ball using only the net. In traditional Iroquois villages, lacrosse was played for fun. But it was also a way to keep young men fit and active for war.

French colonists learned the sport in Canada and spread it throughout the world. Lacrosse even became part of the World Games. But the Iroquois Nationals team was not included in the World Games at first. Finally, in 1990, the team was admitted to the World Games. They took fourth place worldwide in 2002.

CULTURAL LIFE

The Haudenosaunee live modern lives. They work, go to school, and spend time with family. But they also keep alive their cultural traditions, values, and beliefs.

For many centuries, the Mohawk, Oneida, Onondaga, Cayuga, Seneca, and Tuscarora have celebrated the Cycle of Thanksgiving. Modern Haudenosaunee continue the traditions of the cycle and other festivals. The festivals include sacred dancing, chanting, and other rituals.

Haudenosaunee also use festivals and gatherings as a chance to catch up with family and friends. Festivals include social dancing, storytelling, and children's activities. Haudenosaunee food, art, and crafts are usually available.

Members of the Oneida Nation of Wisconsin celebrate their traditions during a summer powwow.

MOHAWK IRONWORKERS

Mohawk ironworkers are well known for their skill. They work hundreds of feet up in the air on large construction projects. They place and weld together huge iron and steel beams on skyscrapers and bridges. Over the past one hundred years, Mohawks have worked on some of the most famous structures in North America. In New York City, they helped build the Empire State Building, the George Washington Bridge, Rockefeller Center, and the World Trade Center.

The people of the Six Nations see the festivals as a way to celebrate their traditions and to pass them on to younger generations.

Haudenosaunee people also continue their traditions through art. Crafters create beadwork, make corn husk dolls, and weave baskets. Painters capture scenes of Haudenosaunee legend, history, and modern life. And sculptors use natural materials, such as stone, deer antler, and clay, to depict Haudenosaunee symbols and clan animals.

Mohawk ironworkers walk the high beams during the construction of a skyscraper in New York City.

Many Haudenosaunee are also working to keep their native languages from dying out. They speak their native languages in their homes. At school, students learn native languages along with English.

INTO THE FUTURE

Like many Native American groups, the Haudenosaunee face the problems of poverty, discrimination, poor education, and lack of good health care.

Government and community leaders find ways to fight these problems. They raise money to build new homes, schools, and clinics and to hire teachers, doctors, and dentists. They bring new businesses into communities to provide jobs for their people.

But the Haudenosaunee also rely on centuries of traditions and beliefs to keep their communities strong. The Six Nations are still united. And the council fire still burns because people still believe in the Great Law of Peace.

An Iroquois elder talks with a boy about his people's traditional culture. By educating the young, the Iroquois keep their traditions alive.

SUCCOTASH

Succotash is a traditional Native American dish. This recipe uses the three sisters of corn, beans, and squash.

> 1 cup frozen or canned corn
> 1 cup frozen or canned lima beans
> 4 slices bacon
> 1 cup chopped (½-inch cubes) summer squash or zucchini
> ½ cup chopped onion
> ½ cup chopped red or green peppers
> ¼ teaspoon ground black pepper
> 1 teaspoon soy sauce
> 1 tablespoon Worcestershire sauce

Thaw frozen vegetables according to package directions. Drain frozen or canned vegetables and set aside. Cut the bacon into 1-inch squares and fry in an uncovered skillet over low heat for 5 minutes, stirring often. Add the squash, onion, and chopped peppers, stirring well to coat the vegetables with the bacon drippings. Cover and cook over medium-high heat for 10 minutes, stirring often enough to keep the vegetables from sticking. Mix in the corn, beans, and all other ingredients. Turn the heat down to medium-low, cover, and cook until the squash is tender, stirring occasionally. Makes 4 to 5 servings.

PLACES TO VISIT

Ganondagan

Victor, New York

(585) 742-1690

http://www.ganondagan.org/

This historic Seneca village includes a full-size replica of a bark longhouse, miles of walking trails, and a huge corn granary. Other exhibits explain Seneca government, food, and medicine.

Iroquois Indian Museum

Howes Cave, New York

(518) 296-8949

http://www.iroquoismuseum.org

Located near Albany, New York, this museum features historic and modern Iroquois art and crafts. Exhibits include basket weaving, sculpture, pottery, beading, and paintings. The museum also includes a forty-five-acre nature park.

Oneida Nation Museum

Oneida, Wisconsin

(920) 869-2768

http://museum.oneidanation.org

This museum focuses on the cultural heritage of the Oneida Nation. Exhibits cover traditional art and crafts and the role of the Oneida in U.S. history.

Six Nations Indian Museum

Onchiota, New York

(518) 891-2299

http://www.tuscaroras.com/graydeer/pages/sixnamus.htm

Dedicated to Haudenosaunee culture, this museum houses modern art and crafts and traditional canoes, baskets, tools, beadwork, feathered headwear, and clothing.

GLOSSARY

ancestors: members of one's family who lived long ago, usually before grandparents

breechcloth: a cloth worn by men to cover the body from the waist to the upper thighs

clan: a group of families all from the same ancestor

confederacy: a union of states, tribes, towns, or people with a common goal

council: a group of people chosen to look after the affairs of a larger group, such as a town or nation

kilt: a type of skirt worn by men

lacrosse: a team game in which each player has a stick with a net on the end. Players use the net to carry, throw, and catch a ball to score points.

leggings: coverings for the legs that usually reach from the thighs to the ankles

longhouse: a type of wooden house built by Native Americans in eastern North America

quill: the long, hollow, central part of a feather. A quill can also be one of the long, pointed spines on a porcupine.

reservation: land set aside by the government for use by Native American communities

sash: a wide strip of leather or cloth worn around the waist or over one shoulder

tradition: a practice, idea, or belief that is handed down from one age to the next

wampum: beads made from polished seashells or glass sewn together into strings and belts

warrior: a soldier, or someone able to fight in battles

FURTHER READING

Bruchac, Joseph. *Children of the Longhouse*. New York: Puffin Books, 1996.
This historical novel tells the story of an eleven-year-old Mohawk
boy, Ohkwa'ri, and his twin sister, Otsi'stia.

Kalman, Bobbie. *Life in a Longhouse Village*. New York: Crabtree
Publishing Company, 2001. This illustrated book details housing,
daily activities, and family life in an Iroquois village.

Kirk, Connie A. *The Mohawk of North America*. Minneapolis: Lerner
Publications Company, 2001. Kirk focuses on Mohawk culture,
history, and contemporary life.

Tehanetorens. *Legends of the Iroquois*. Summertown, TN: Book Publishing
Company, 1998. Master storyteller Tehanetorens recounts Iroquois
myths and legends. The book is illustrated by Kahionhes,
Tehanetorens's son.

WEBSITES

Official Homepage of the Haudenosaunee
http://www.sixnations.org
This home page provides news and information about the
Haudenosaunee, including culture and beliefs, the workings of the
government, and the Great Law of Peace.

Official Website of the Oneida Nation of Wisconsin
http://www.oneidanation.org
The Oneida of Wisconsin's website includes information on history,
cultural traditions, clan responsibilities, government, and current news.

The Seneca Nation of Indians
http://www.sni.org
The official website of the Seneca of New York provides news,
government information, maps of Seneca reservations, and more.

SELECTED BIBLIOGRAPHY

Appleton Public Library. "The Lost Dauphin." *Appleton History*. May 21, 2004. http://www.apl.org/history/dauphin.html (February 2005).

George-Kanentiio, Doug. "How Much Land Did the Iroquois Possess?" *Akwesasne Notes New Series*, vol. 1, no. 3–4 (Fall 1995): 60.

George-Kanentiio, Doug. "Iroquois Population in 1995." *Akwesasne Notes New Series*, vol. 1, no. 3–4 (Fall 1995): 61.

Hoxie, Frederick E., ed. *Encyclopedia of North American Indians*. New York: Houghton Mifflin Company, 1996.

Johansen, Bruce E. "Dating the Iroquois Confederacy." *Akwesasne Notes New Series*, vol. 1, no. 3–4 (Fall 1995): 62–63.

Milwaukee Public Museum. *Indian Country Wisconsin*. N.d. http://www.mpm.edu/wirp/ (February 2005).

Redish, Laura. *Native Languages of the Americas: Iroquoian Language Family*. N.d. http://www.native-languages.org/famiro.htm (February 2005).

Schiffert, Vince. *Lacrosse*. N.d. http://www.nw.wnyric.org/tuscarora/tuscaroraschool/lacrosse.htm (February 2005).

Seaver, James. *A Narrative of the Life of Mrs. Mary Jemison*. Rev. ed. New York: American Scenic and Historical Preservation Society, 1942.

Thomae, Dawn Scher. "Wisconsin Warriors: Interviews with Native American Veterans." *LORE* (Milwaukee Public Museum) 43, no. 3 (September 1993): 9–18.

Weatherford, Jack. *Indian Givers: How the Indians of the Americas Transformed the World*. New York: Ballantine Books, 1988.

INDEX